Kinkajous

by Rachel Lynette

Consultant:
Dr. Mark C. Andersen
Department of Fish, Wildlife and Conservation Ecology
New Mexico State University

BEARPORT
PUBLISHING

New York, New York

Credits

Cover and Title, © Amazon-Images/Alamy; 4–5, © Aldo Brando/Peter Arnold/Getty Images; 6, © Red Line Editorial; 6–7, 22 (middle), © ZSSD/SuperStock 8, © Red Line Editorial; 8–9, © NHPA/SuperStock; 10–11, © Exactostock/SuperStock; 12–13, © Carol Farneti Foster/Oxford Scientific/Getty Images; 14–15, © Joe McDonald/Visuals Unlimited/Getty Images; 16, © Karen Givens/Shutterstock Images; 16–17, © Tom Boyden/Lonely Planet Images/Getty Images; 18, 22 (bottom), © Arvind Balaraman/Shutterstock Images; 18–19, © NHPA/SuperStock; 20–21, © age fotostock/SuperStock; 22 (top), © NHPA/SuperStock; 22 (middle), © NHPA/SuperStock; 23 (top), © Aldo Brando/Peter Arnold/Getty Images; 23 (middle), © Karen Givens/Shutterstock Images; 23 (bottom), © NHPA/SuperStock.

Publisher: Kenn Goin
Editor: Joy Bean
Creative Director: Spencer Brinker
Photo Researcher: Arnold Ringstad
Design: Emily Love

Library of Congress Cataloging-in-Publication Data in process at time of publication (2013)
Library of Congress Control Number: 2012039857
ISBN-13: 978-1-61772-752-8 (library binding)

For more information, write to Bearport Publishing Company, Inc., 45 West 21st Street, Suite 3B, New York, New York 10010. Printed in the United States of America.

10 9 8 7 6 5 4 3 2 1

Contents

Meet a kinkajou

A young kinkajou swings between the trees in the **rain forest**.

Even though it is nighttime, the kinkajou has left its home to look for food.

Kinkajous are sometimes called night walkers because they are **nocturnal**.

Tonight, the kinkajou hopes to find some ripe fruit to eat.

kinkajou

What is a kinkajou?

Kinkajous are small **mammals** that are related to raccoons.

They have thick brown fur, large eyes, and small ears.

Their most noticeable feature, however, is their long, powerful tail.

Their tails are about 20 inches (51 cm) long, the same length as their bodies.

Adult kinkajou size

Kinkajou homes

Kinkajous live in the rain forests of Mexico and Central and South America.

They spend most of their time in the tops of trees.

☐ **Where kinkajous live**

North America

Mexico

Atlantic Ocean

Central America

South America

Pacific Ocean

They eat, sleep, and play on the branches.

They hardly ever go down to the ground.

Useful features

Kinkajous' sharp claws help them climb trees quickly.

Once high in a tree, adult kinkajous use their tails like another arm.

They hang from branches and swing from tree to tree.

tail

claws

A baby kinkajou

When a mother kinkajou is ready to give birth, she crawls into a tree hole.

She has just one **kit** at a time.

It weighs about six ounces (170 g) when born, a little bit more than a baseball.

The mother feeds the baby milk from her body to help it grow stronger.

mother kinkajou

baby kinkajou

13

Protecting the baby

The mother kinkajou keeps her kit close for the first eight weeks of its life.

When she has to leave the tree hole, she carries her baby on her belly.

If a baby kinkajou feels scared, it makes a hissing noise.

If there is no danger, the mother will calm her baby by chirping softly.

However, if **predators** are nearby, she will race to get her baby to safety.

tree hole

15

Time to sleep

When the sun comes up, kinkajous find a tree hole to sleep in.

They stay asleep all day.

The hole keeps the animals hidden and safe while predators, such as jaguars, are awake.

jaguar

kinkajou resting
in tree hole

17

Finding food

When a kit is 12 weeks old, it starts helping its mother look for food.

Kinkajous mostly eat fruit, but they also like honey, **nectar**, frogs, and insects.

They are also known as honey bears because they love honey so much.

nectar

Leaving home

When a kinkajou is four months old, it is fully grown.

It can find its own food and hang by its tail.

adult
kinkajou

When she is two years old, a female kinkajou can have a baby.

At about that time, she will leave her mother.

She will swing away one night to start a family of her own.

Glossary

kit (KIT)
the baby of an animal such as a kinkajou

mammals (MAM-uhls)
warm-blooded animals that drink their mother's milk as babies

nectar (NEK-tur)
a sweet liquid made by plants

nocturnal (nok-TUR-nuhl)
active only at night

predators (PRED-uh-turz)
animals that hunt and
eat other animals

rain forest (RAYN FOR-ist)
a large, warm area of
land covered with trees
and plants, where lots of
rain falls

Index

Read more

Amstutz, Lisa Jo. *Rain Forest Animal Adaptations (Amazing Animal Adaptations).* North Mankato, MN: Capstone (2012).

Petrie, Kristin. *Kinkajous (Nocturnal Animals).* Minneapolis, MN: ABDO (2010).

Learn more online

To learn more about kinkajous, visit
www.bearportpublishing.com/JungleBabies

About the author

Rachel Lynette has written more than 100 nonfiction books for children. She also creates resources for teachers. Rachel lives near Seattle, Washington. She enjoys biking, hiking, crocheting hats, and spending time with her family and friends.